THE DAYS ARE JUST PACKED

Other Books by Bill Watterson

Calvin and Hobbes
Something Under the Bed Is Drooling
Yukon Ho!
Weirdos from Another Planet
The Revenge of the Baby-Sat
Scientific Progress Goes "Boink"
Attack of the Deranged Mutant Killer Monster Snow Goons
Homicidal Psycho Jungle Cat
There's Treasure Everywhere
It's a Magical World

Treasury Collections

The Essential Calvin and Hobbes
The Calvin and Hobbes Lazy Sunday Book
The Authoritative Calvin and Hobbes
The Indispensable Calvin and Hobbes
The Calvin and Hobbes 10th Anniversary Book

THE DAYS ARE JUST PACKED

A Calvin and Hobbes Collection by Bill Watterson

**Andrews McMeel
Publishing, LLC**

Kansas City

ISBN-13: 978-0-7407-7797-4
ISBN-10: 0-7407-7797-1

www.andrewsmcmeel.com

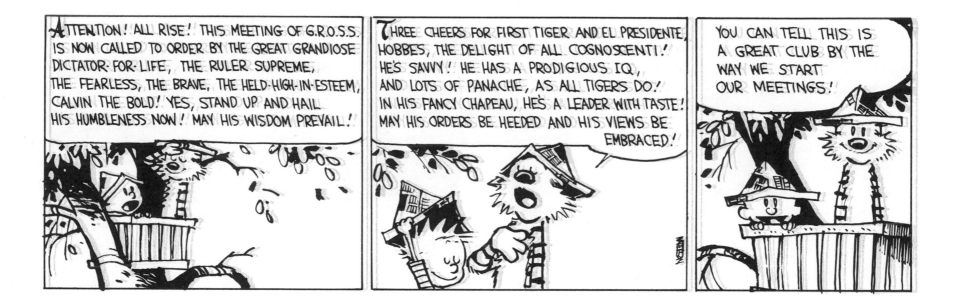

15

HELP HELP! MY HEAD SOMEHOW GOT TWISTED COMPLETELY AROUND! I'M FACING BACKWARD!

LOOK! I CAN READ THE TAG ON MY SHIRT! I CAN SEE DOWN MY OWN BACK!

...OH, WAIT. THERE'S MY BELLY BUTTON. I MUST JUST HAVE MY *SHIRT* ON BACKWARD.

NEVER MIND. I'VE GOT MY HEAD ON STRAIGHT AFTER ALL.

OH, I WOULDN'T GO *THAT* FAR.

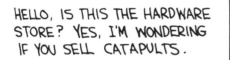

43

49

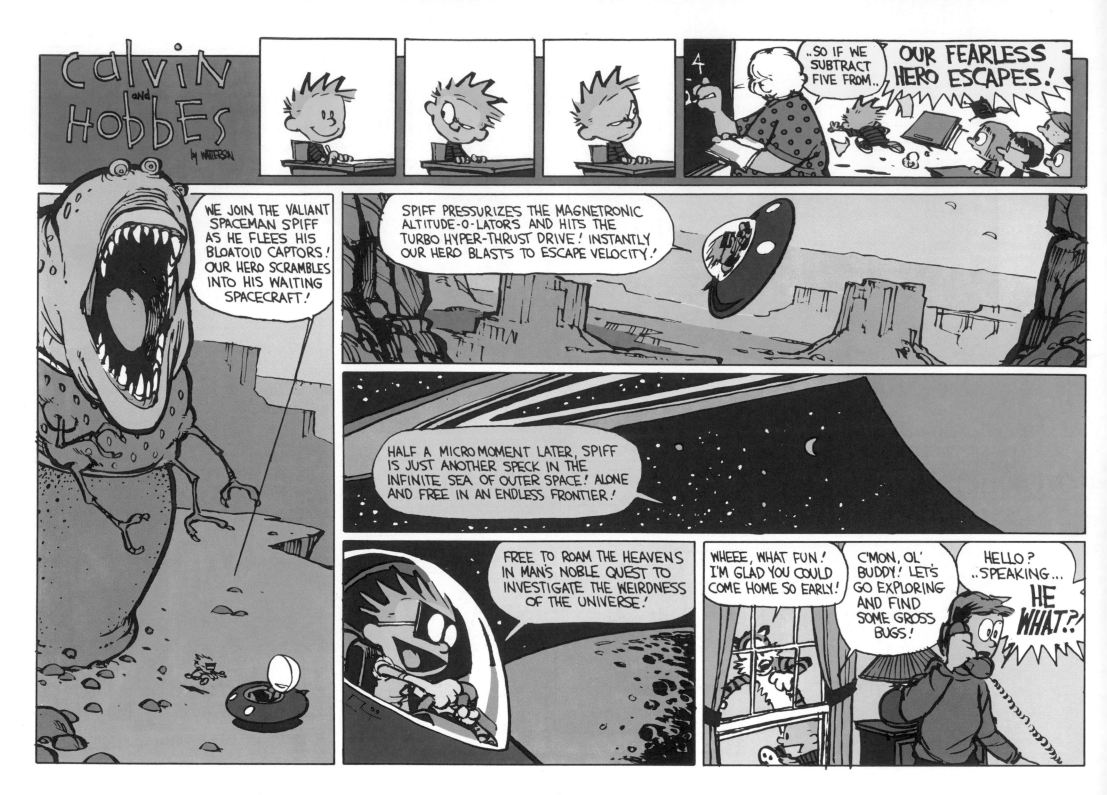

50

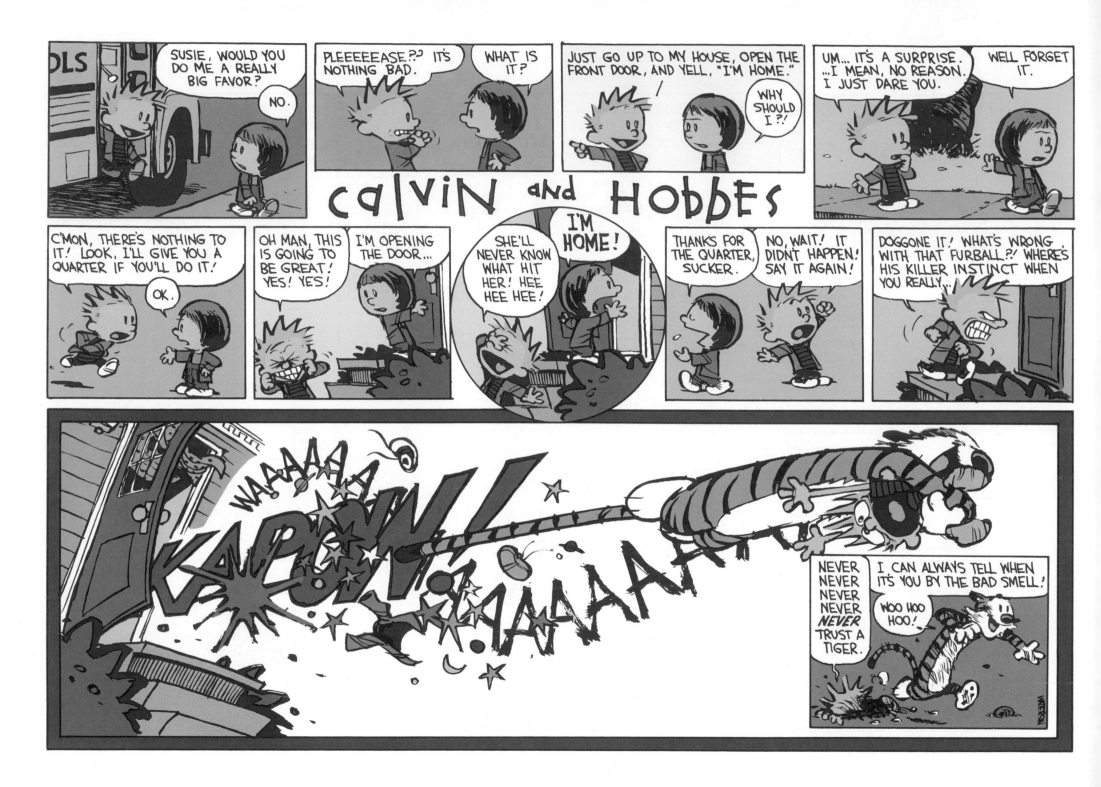

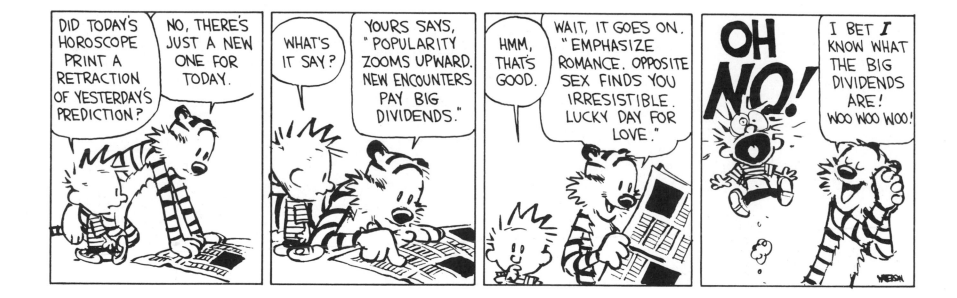

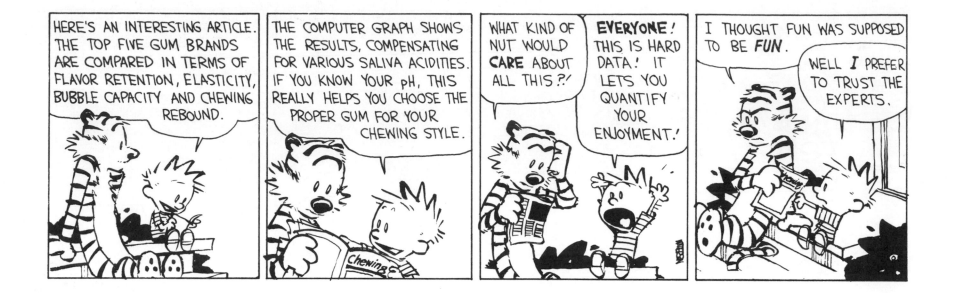

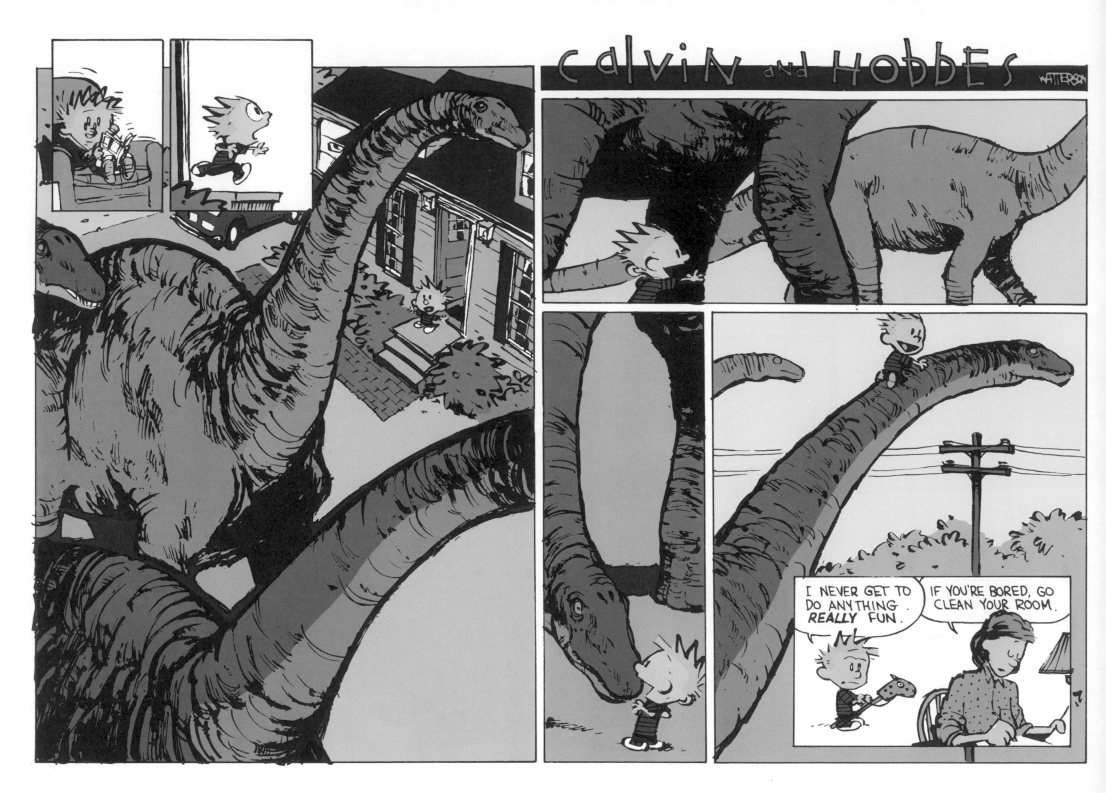

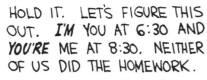

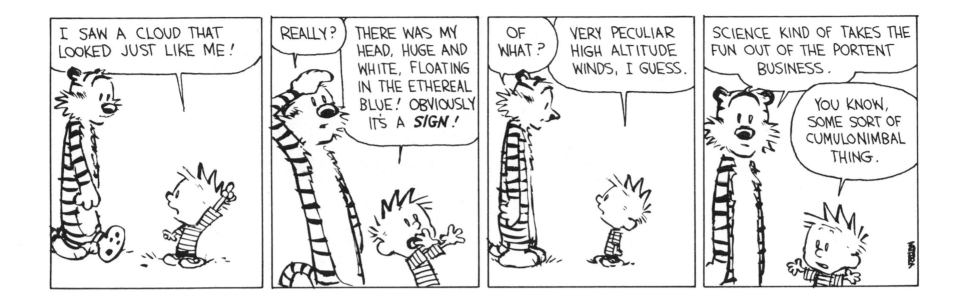

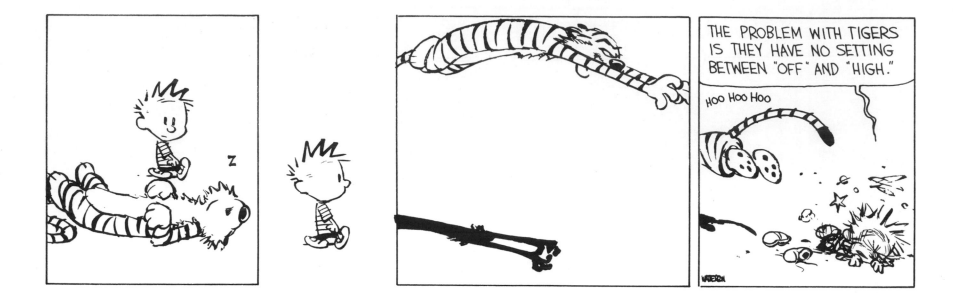

126

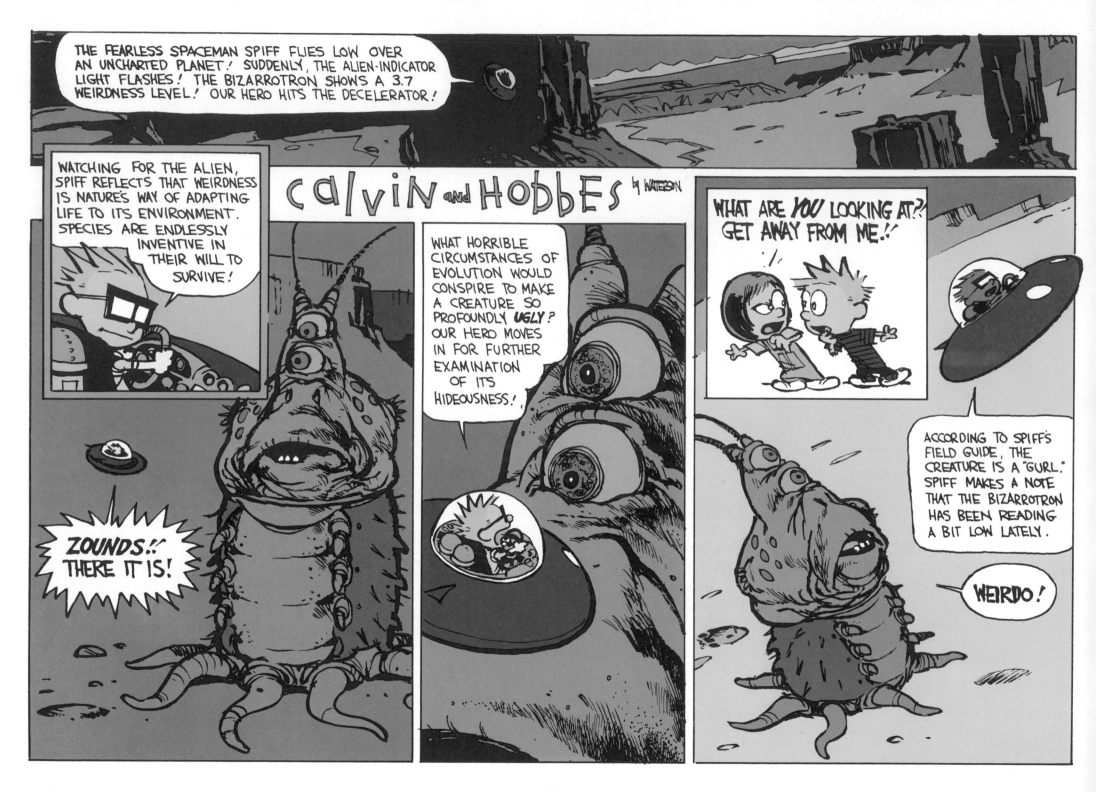

140

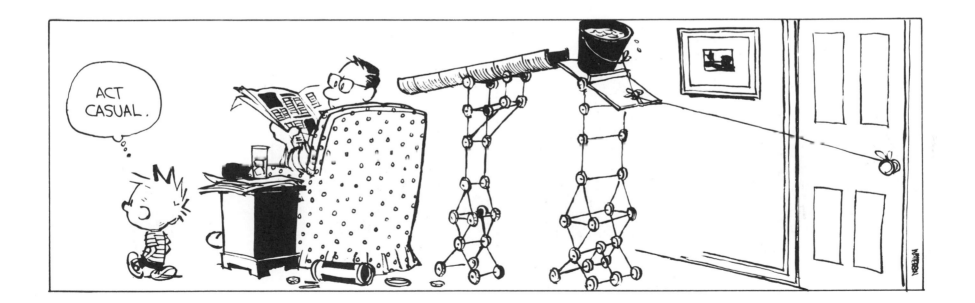